HOLIDAY TREATS

EASY RECIPES FOR PARTIES, TREATS, AND GIFTS

table of contents

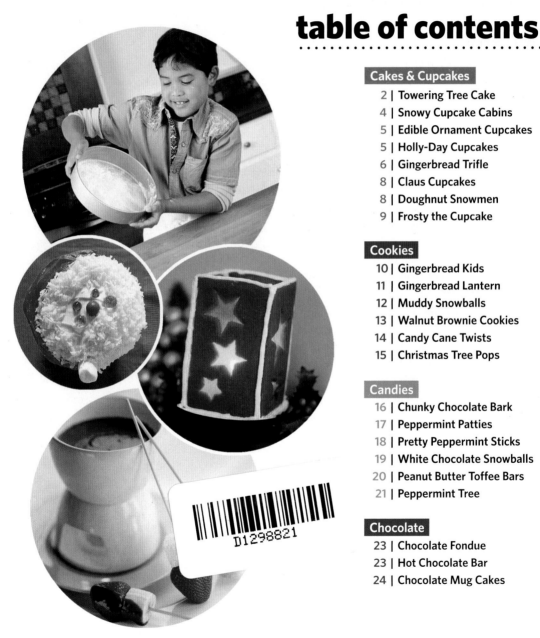

D1298821

© Meredith Corporation. For more great ideas, subscribe to *FamilyFun* magazine by calling 800-289-4849 or going to FamilyFunmag.com
Published in 2012 by Dalmatian Press, LLC. Printed in China.
The DALMATIAN PRESS name is a trademark of Dalmatian Press, LLC, Franklin, Tennessee 37067. 1-866-418-2572.

towering tree cake

TOTAL TIME: 1 HOUR (after cake bakes and cools) | **SERVES:** 18–20

Want your holiday dinner to end on a sweet note? Finish it off with this creative Christmas tree complete with candy ornaments, an icing garland, and (of course) presents!

YOU WILL NEED

- ❏ 1 (18.25-ounce) box yellow or white cake mix
- ❏ Parchment paper or aluminum foil
- ❏ 12-inch wooden skewer
- ❏ 3¾ cups confectioners' sugar
- ❏ 4½ tablespoons water

- ❏ 3 teaspoons vanilla, peppermint, or lemon extract
- ❏ Food coloring in green and other colors
- ❏ Candies for ornaments (we used Wonka Runts)
- ❏ 1 tube yellow decorators' icing (not gel)

1. Prepare the cake mix according to the package directions using an electric mixer (this yields a firmer cake). Bake in a 9- by 13-inch pan lined with parchment paper or foil. Let the cake cool completely.

2. Place the cake on a cutting board and use a long, sharp knife (parents only) to shave off the rounded top. Carefully flip over the cake and cut it into 7 squares, as shown, setting the extra aside. Cut the bottom half off each of the 2 smallest squares and set them aside with the other leftover cake pieces.

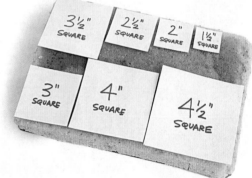

3. Stack the cake squares from largest to smallest on a serving platter, setting each one at a 45-degree angle to the one below it. Trim the skewer so that it's just slightly shorter than the cake and stick it down through the stack to help keep the squares together.

4. To prepare the icing, stir together the confectioners' sugar, water, and extract in a medium bowl until smooth (it should be about the consistency of honey). Set aside ½ cup of the mixture. Tint the remaining icing with the green food coloring until it reaches a shade you like (we used about 12 drops).

5. Pour the tinted icing over the cake from the top, using a rubber spatula or butter knife to gently spread it over the cake as needed.

6. To make the presents, divide the remaining icing among 2 or 3 bowls and tint each with a different color of food coloring. Cut the extra cake pieces into small squares. Set them on a wire rack with a plate or wax paper underneath. Pour the icing over the squares. Let the icing set for a few minutes. Use a spatula to carefully move the presents to the base of the tree.

7. Decorate the tree with candy ornaments and use the tube of decorators' icing to add a frosting garland to the tree and frosting ribbons and bows to the gifts. To serve, remove and cut the layers one at a time.

snowy cupcake cabins

TOTAL TIME: 20 MINUTES (after cupcakes bake and cool) | **MAKES:** 12 CUPCAKES

With cookie chimneys and candy holiday lights, these snowy cupcakes look like just the sort of hideaway Santa's elves might live in.

YOU WILL NEED

- ❏ 12 cupcakes (or mix)
- ❏ 8 ounces cream cheese, softened
- ❏ 2 tablespoons butter, softened
- ❏ 2 cups confectioners' sugar
- ❏ Sweetened flaked coconut (optional)
- ❏ ¾ teaspoon vanilla extract
- ❏ Pepperidge Farm Pirouette cookies
- ❏ M&M's Minis

1. Prepare your favorite cupcake batter and bake it in a muffin pan lined with paper bake cups. While the cupcakes cool, mix the cream cheese frosting. Using an electric mixer, beat together the cream cheese, softened butter, confectioners' sugar, and a pinch of salt until smooth and creamy. Blend in the vanilla extract. Chill the frosting while you complete step two.

2. With permanent colored markers, have your child draw windows and doors on 12 empty paper bake cups. (It's easier if you keep the cups stacked and draw on the outer one rather than on the individual cups.)

3. Dab frosting inside each decorated cup (3 or 4 spots spaced equally apart and about ⅓ inch down from the top should do it). Fit the decorated cups over the ones the cupcakes were baked in, pressing gently so the frosting adheres the 2 layers together.

4. Spread frosting on each cupcake, heaping it in the center to resemble a peaked, snow-covered roof. Carefully press on sweetened flaked coconut, if desired. For a chimney, gently but firmly push half of a Pepperidge Farm Pirouette cookie into the cake. Finally, add M&M's Minis holiday lights around the roof's perimeter.

edible ornament cupcake

TOTAL TIME: 20 MINUTES (after cupcakes bake and cool)

These delectable decorations are just the treat for a holiday tree-trimming party.

YOU WILL NEED

- ❏ Cupcakes
- ❏ Colorful frosting
- ❏ Decorators' gel
- ❏ Red and green (we used M&M's Minis)
- ❏ Mini Reese's Peanut Butter Cups
- ❏ Pretzels

1. Frost a batch of cooled cupcakes with colorful frosting.

2. Decorate with gel icing and candies (we used red and green M&M's Minis). Top each one with a miniature Reese's Peanut Butter Cup and a pretzel piece for an ornament hanger. Don't forget to save one for Santa!

holly-day cupcakes

TOTAL TIME: 20 MINUTES (after cupcakes bake and cool)

'Tis the season when you're sure to need a special dessert to bring to a Christmas party or school bake sale.

YOU WILL NEED

- ❏ Cupcakes
- ❏ White icing
- ❏ Shredded coconut
- ❏ Green gumdrops
- ❏ Sugar, for sprinkling gumdrop leaves
- ❏ Red candy for holly berries (we used M&M's Minis)
- ❏ Wax paper

1. Frost the cupcakes with snowy white icing and top with shredded coconut.

2. Use a rolling pin to flatten green gumdrops on a piece of wax paper sprinkled with sugar. Use a butter knife to cut out holly leaf shapes.

3. Arrange two or three leaves and a few red candy "berries" on top of each cupcake, pressing them into the frosting just enough to hold them in place.

gingerbread trifle

TOTAL TIME: 1 HOUR, 55 MINUTES (plus chill time) | **SERVES: 18**

Our version of this classic English confection is a festive feast for the eyes as well as the mouth. The luscious layers of gingerbread cake, vanilla custard, raspberries, and whipped cream form a dramatic dessert that stacks up in taste.

YOU WILL NEED

FOR THE GINGERBREAD
- ❑ 1½ teaspoons baking soda
- ❑ 2½ cups flour
- ❑ 1 teaspoon ground cinnamon
- ❑ 1 teaspoon ground ginger
- ❑ ½ teaspoon salt
- ❑ ½ cup butter, slightly softened
- ❑ ½ cup sugar
- ❑ ¾ cup dark molasses
- ❑ 2 large eggs, at room temperature
- ❑ ¾ cup buttermilk

FOR THE CUSTARD
- ❑ 9 large eggs
- ❑ ¾ cup sugar
- ❑ ¼ cup flour
- ❑ 3 cups whole milk
- ❑ 1¼ teaspoons vanilla extract

FOR THE FILLING
- ❑ 3 (12-ounce) packages frozen unsweetened raspberries, thawed and drained
- ❑ 1 cup chilled heavy cream
- ❑ 3 tablespoons sugar
- ❑ 2 teaspoons confectioners' sugar
- ❑ ½ pint fresh raspberries

FOR THE GINGERBREAD

1. Heat the oven to 350°. Generously grease and flour a 9-inch round cake pan. In a small bowl, whisk together the flour, baking soda, ginger, cinnamon, and salt.

2. In a large bowl with an electric mixer set on medium-high speed, beat the butter until it's soft and creamy, about 1 minute. Use a spatula to scrape down the sides of the bowl. Add the sugar and molasses and beat again until the mixture is well blended and fluffy, about 2 minutes more. Add the eggs one at a time, beating 30 seconds after each addition. Slowly pour in the buttermilk and beat well. Reduce the mixer's speed to low, slowly add half the flour mixture to the bowl, and beat until blended. Repeat with the other half.

3. Pour the batter into the cake pan. Bake until a wooden toothpick inserted into the center of the cake comes out clean, about 45 minutes. Let the cake cool completely on a wire rack. Cover it tightly with plastic wrap until ready to use. It can be stored in the pan at room temperature for up to two days.

FOR THE CUSTARD

1. Divide the egg yolks and whites by carefully tipping each yolk back and forth between the shell halves, letting the whites spill into a bowl. Place the yolks in a separate bowl. In a large bowl with an electric mixer set on medium-high speed, beat the yolks and sugar until the mixture is pale yellow and thick, about 2 to 3 minutes. Reduce the speed to low and beat in the flour.

2. In a medium saucepan, bring the milk to a boil. Slowly pour half the milk into the egg mixture and beat until blended. Pour the mixture into the remaining milk in the pan. Over medium heat, bring the ingredients to a boil while whisking constantly. Allow the custard to boil for 1 minute as you continue to whisk. Remove the pan from the heat and stir in the vanilla.

3. Let the custard cool slightly and cover its surface with plastic wrap to prevent a skin from forming. Let the custard cool completely and refrigerate it until ready to use (up to three days).

TO ASSEMBLE THE TRIFLE

1. In a medium bowl, toss the thawed raspberries and sugar. Remove the gingerbread from the pan and use a serrated knife to slice it into four equal wedges. Turn each wedge on its side and slice it into three equal pieces. Stack them, slice the pile in half, and cut off 1½ inches from the tips, reserving the pieces.

2. Arrange a layer of six cake wedges over the bottom of a 2½-quart bowl. Fill the center with a few of the trimmings. Spoon and spread ¾ cup of the raspberry mixture over the cake. Top the fruit with 1 cup of custard. Repeat the layering three more times with the remaining ingredients. Cover the bowl with plastic wrap and refrigerate it for at least 3 hours (but overnight is best) to let the flavors meld.

3. Before serving, make the whipped cream. In a medium bowl with an electric mixer on medium-high speed, whip the cream with the confectioners' sugar until soft peaks form, about 3 minutes. Use a spatula to spread the whipped cream on top of the trifle and garnish it with the fresh raspberries.

claus cupcakes

TOTAL TIME: 10 MINUTES (after cupcakes bake and cool)

Heading down the chimney? Be careful how many of these tempting Santa cupcakes you eat!

YOU WILL NEED
- ❑ Cupcakes
- ❑ White and red icing
- ❑ Mini marshmallows
- ❑ Shredded coconut
- ❑ Blue and pink gel icing
- ❑ Red candies

1. Frost the cupcake with a layer of white icing. Add the red frosting hat, curving it around the side of Santa's face, and a marshmallow pom-pom.

2. Sprinkle on a ring of coconut to make Santa's beard and hair. Draw his eyes and cheeks with gel icing. Top it all off with a red candy nose.

doughnut snowmen

TIME: 10 MINUTES

No snow? No problem. Whether you live in a Sun Belt state or a wintry clime, your kids can easily build their own mini versions of Frosty.

YOU WILL NEED
- ❑ Small powdered doughnuts
- ❑ Powdered doughnut holes
- ❑ Decorators' gel
- ❑ Pretzel or potato sticks
- ❑ Haviland Thin Mints
- ❑ Reese's peanut butter cup miniatures

1. Set a powdered doughnut hole atop a mini powdered doughnut.
(For a taller version, use a pretzel stick or a potato stick to secure a second doughnut hole atop the first.)

2. Use decorators' gel to add a face, buttons, and a carrot nose. (If the gel won't stick, try smoothing the powder with a dab of water first.)

3. To add a top hat to a shorter snowman, stick a small piece of a pretzel or potato stick through a Haviland Thin Mint and into a Reese's peanut butter cup miniature, then secure the hat in place on the snowman.

frosty the cupcake

TOTAL TIME: 10 MINUTES (after cupcakes bake and cool)

Heading down the chimney? Be careful how many of these tempting Santa cupcakes you eat!

YOU WILL NEED
- ❏ Cupcakes
- ❏ White icing
- ❏ Large marshmallows
- ❏ Wax paper
- ❏ Pretzel sticks
- ❏ Decorators' gel
- ❏ Orange slice candy
- ❏ Junior Mints
- ❏ Thin Mints
- ❏ Fruit leather

1. Frost a cooled cupcake (baked from your favorite recipe) with white icing.

2. Flatten a large marshmallow on wax paper with the palm of your hand. Cut a second marshmallow in half horizontally, then stack the halves on the first marshmallow to form a torso and head.

3. Push a thin pretzel stick down through the snowman (this will help him stand up), then set him on the cupcake.

4. Use decorators' gel to create a mouth, eyes, and buttons. Add pretzel stick arms and a wedge cut from an orange slice candy for a nose.

5. Accessorize with a candy hat (a Junior Mint secured to a Thin Mint with icing) and a fruit leather scarf.

gingerbread kids

TOTAL TIME: 1 HOUR (plus chill time) | **MAKES:** 25 COOKIES

It wouldn't be Christmas without the chance to dress gingerbread cookies in frosting finery.

Cookies

YOU WILL NEED

- ❏ 4½ cups all-purpose flour
- ❏ 1 tablespoon ground cinnamon
- ❏ 2 teaspoons ground ginger
- ❏ ¼ teaspoon ground cloves
- ❏ 1¼ teaspoons baking soda
- ❏ ½ cup butter, softened
- ❏ ½ cup packed brown sugar
- ❏ 2 large eggs
- ❏ ¾ cup molasses
- ❏ White decorators' frosting
- ❏ Red and green M&M's and Skittles
- ❏ Cookie cutter

1. In a medium-sized bowl, sift the flour, cinnamon, ginger, cloves, and baking soda. Set aside dry ingredients.

2. In a large bowl, blend the butter and brown sugar. Add the eggs, one at a time, and then the molasses. Slowly add the flour mixture to the molasses mixture, stirring after each addition with the wooden spoon or mixer (the dough should be stiff).

3. Divide the dough in half, flatten into a thick pancake (a fun step for kids set up with a rolling pin), and cover with plastic wrap. Refrigerate for 2 hours, or until the dough is firm enough to roll (if it becomes too stiff, soften for 10 minutes at room temperature).

4. Preheat the oven to 350°. On a floured counter, roll out the dough to a ¼-inch thickness. Use a cookie cutter to cut out gingerbread men and a flat spatula to transfer them to a greased cookie sheet, spacing them 1 inch apart. Bake for 10 minutes, or until light brown.

5. Once the gingerbread men have cooled, invite your kids to pipe on frosting faces and clothing. Add red and green candies for buttons.

gingerbread lantern

TOTAL TIME: 90 MINUTES (plus cool times) | **MAKES:** 1 LANTERN

You and your family can shed new light on a holiday baking tradition with this festive gingerbread lantern.

YOU WILL NEED

FOR THE GINGERBREAD

- ❏ ⅓ cup butter, room temperature
- ❏ ⅓ cup sugar
- ❏ ½ teaspoon baking soda
- ❏ 4 teaspoons water
- ❏ ⅓ cup molasses
- ❏ 1⅔ cups flour, plus extra for rolling
- ❏ 1¼ teaspoons ginger
- ❏ ¼ teaspoon allspice
- ❏ ½ teaspoon cinnamon
- ❏ Hard candies (we used Jolly Rancher Candies)
- ❏ Parchment paper
- ❏ Cookie cutters

FOR THE THE ICING

- ❏ 1½ cups confectioners' sugar
- ❏ 1 tablespoon meringue powder
- ❏ 2 to 3 tablespoons warm water

1. To make the gingerbread, heat the oven to 350°. In a large bowl, beat the butter and the sugar with an electric mixer on medium-high speed for about 5 minutes. Stir the baking soda into the water to dissolve it, then add to the butter mixture. Stir in the molasses. Combine the flour, ginger, allspice, and cinnamon in a medium bowl. Stir the dry ingredients into the butter mixture a little at a time. Cover the bowl with plastic wrap and chill for 1 hour.

2. Prepare the lantern's four sides by rolling out the chilled dough to a ¼-inch thickness on a large piece of parchment paper, sprinkling on some flour if the dough sticks. Then, using a 4- by 7-inch piece of cardboard as a template, cut 4 rectangles from the dough, removing any scraps. Transfer the gingerbread pieces to a cookie sheet by topping them first with a piece of parchment paper the size of the cookie sheet, then with the inverted cookie sheet itself. Quickly flip everything over and remove the top piece of parchment paper.

3. To install the windows, use cookie cutters dipped in flour to cut and remove a few shapes from each gingerbread piece. Unwrap candies in similar colors (you'll need about 2 to 3 for each 2½-inch cutout) and place them in doubled freezer bags. Hit them gently with a hammer to crush them, then generously fill each cutout with crushed candy. Bake the gingerbread for 12 minutes, then let it cool for at least 1 hour. The candy windows will be extremely hot! Do not touch them until they have cooled completely.

4. Finally, construct the lantern by beating together all of the icing ingredients in a small bowl with an electric mixer on low speed until blended, then increase the speed to high and beat for 4 to 5 minutes or until stiff peaks form. Using a pastry bag or a plastic bag with a corner cut off, pipe icing along the long edges of 2 of the walls. Assemble all 4 walls vertically on a platter or a piece of foil-covered cardboard, filling in any gaps and decorating the edges with more icing. Allow the icing to dry overnight. Set the lantern in a safe spot, then place an LED flameless tea light inside and enjoy!

muddy snowballs

TIME: 60 MINUTES (plus 1–2 hours chill time) | **MAKES:** 48

Chocolate lovers will devour this cocoa version of snowballs, the classic holiday cookie.

YOU WILL NEED

FOR THE COOKIES

❑ 1 cup (2 sticks) unsalted butter, softened

❑ 2 ounces unsweetened chocolate, melted and cooled

❑ ⅔ cup confectioner's sugar

❑ 1 egg yolk

❑ 1½ teaspoons vanilla extract

❑ 2 cups all-purpose flour

❑ ¼ teaspoon salt

❑ ¾ cup finely chopped walnuts

FOR THE DUST

❑ ¾ cup confectioners' sugar

❑ 3 tablespoons unsweetened cocoa powder

1. In a large bowl, use a wooden spoon to cream the butter until smooth. Stir in the melted chocolate and blend well.

2. Add the confectioners' sugar, egg yolk, and vanilla extract and stir until combined. Stir in the flour and salt until smooth.

3. Add the walnuts and stir until combined. Cover and refrigerate the dough for at least 1 to 2 hours, or until firm enough to roll into balls.

4. Heat the oven to 350°. Form scant tablespoonfuls of the dough into 1-inch balls. Place the balls on two ungreased baking sheets, leaving about 1 inch between them. Bake for 10 to 12 minutes or until the tops of the cookies are set. Cool on the baking sheets for about 3 minutes. Repeat until all the dough has been used.

5. Meanwhile, stir together the ¾ cup confectioners' sugar and cocoa powder in a shallow bowl. Carefully dip the warm cookies into the dust to coat as they come out of the oven.

6. Cool the cookies completely on a wire rack. Roll again in the cocoa-confectioners' sugar dust. Store in an airtight container.

walnut brownie cookies

TOTAL TIME: 1 HOUR (plus chill time) | **MAKES:** 24–30 COOKIES

You'll be nuts about these moist, fudgy creations that make a great holiday treat.

YOU WILL NEED

- ❏ ½ cup unsalted butter, softened
- ❏ 6 ounces unsweetened chocolate, coarsely chopped
- ❏ 2 cups sugar
- ❏ 4 large eggs, at room temperature
- ❏ 2 teaspoons vanilla extract
- ❏ 1 cup walnut pieces or halves
- ❏ 2 cups flour
- ❏ 2 teaspoons baking powder
- ❏ ½ teaspoon salt
- ❏ Confectioners' sugar, for coating

1. In the top of a double boiler, melt together the butter and chocolate over very low heat. Remove the inner pan and allow the mixture to partially cool, then stir it until smooth.

2. In a bowl, beat the sugar and eggs with an electric mixer at high speed until light and airy, about 4 to 5 minutes. Blend in the vanilla extract and partially cooled chocolate. Chop the walnuts very finely (a food processor works well for this) and stir them into the chocolate mixture.

3. Sift the flour, baking powder, and salt into a medium bowl. Stir the dry ingredients into the chocolate mixture half at a time, until the dough is evenly mixed—it will be quite soft. Cover and refrigerate the dough for 3-4 hours.

4. Heat the oven to 325°. Grease 2 large cookie sheets or line them with parchment paper. Put about 1 cup of confectioners' sugar in a small bowl. Shape the dough into 1½-inch-thick balls. Generously coat each one with confectioners' sugar and place it on a baking sheet, leaving about 3 inches between cookies. Bake the cookies on the center rack 1 sheet at a time for about 13 minutes. When done, the cookies will have puffed and will feel very soft to the touch. Do not overbake.

5. Cool the cookies on the cookie sheet for 15 minutes, then transfer them to a wire rack to cool completely.

candy cane twists

TIME: 80 MINUTES | MAKES: 18

These colorful treats offer a clever twist on the classic sugar cookie. Peppermint extract adds that authentic candy cane flavor.

YOU WILL NEED

- ❏ 1 cup unsalted butter, softened
- ❏ ¾ cup sugar
- ❏ 1 large egg
- ❏ 1½ teaspoons vanilla extract
- ❏ 1 teaspoon peppermint extract
- ❏ ½ cup butter, slightly softened
- ❏ ¼ teaspoon salt
- ❏ 2½ cups flour
- ❏ ½ teaspoon red food coloring
- ❏ ½ teaspoon green food coloring

1. Using an electric mixer set on medium-high speed, cream the butter. Continue beating and gradually add the sugar.

2. Beat in the egg until evenly mixed, then add the vanilla extract, the peppermint extract, and the salt and blend well.

3. Use a wooden spoon to stir in the flour, one third at a time, until evenly mixed.

4. Divide the dough into thirds. Add the red food coloring to one third and the green food coloring to another, then knead the coloring into the dough. Flatten each third into a ½-inch-thick rectangle, cover it in plastic wrap, and refrigerate until firm, about 30 minutes.

5. Heat the oven to 375°. On a lightly floured surface, roll a pair of tablespoon-size pieces of contrasting colored dough into 8-inch-long ropes. Twist them together, pinch the ends, then bend the cookies into a candy cane shape. Repeat with the remaining dough.

6. Bake the cookies on an ungreased cookie sheet until set but not brown, about 10 minutes, rotating the sheet halfway through. Cool the sheets on a wire rack for 5 minutes, then transfer the cookies to the rack to continue cooling.

christmas tree pops

TIME: 1 HOUR (Plus overnight cooling time) | **MAKES:** 5 DOZEN

Decorating Christmas tree pops will keep the little elves in your family busy.

YOU WILL NEED

- ❏ 1 cup unsalted butter, softened
- ❏ ¾ cup sugar
- ❏ 1 large egg
- ❏ 1 teaspoon vanilla extract or ½ teaspoon of lemon or almond extract
- ❏ ¼ teaspoon salt
- ❏ 2½ cups flour
- ❏ Green decorators' frosting
- ❏ M&M's minis
- ❏ Craft sticks

1. Using an electric mixer at medium-high speed, cream the butter, gradually adding the sugar. Beat in the egg until evenly mixed, then blend in the vanilla (or lemon or almond extract) and salt.

2. With a wooden spoon, stir the flour into the creamed ingredients, about one third at a time, until evenly blended. The dough may seem soft, but it will firm up when refrigerated.

3. Divide the dough in half. Flatten each portion into a disk about ¾-inch thick and seal in plastic wrap. Refrigerate overnight.

4. Remove the dough from the refrigerator and let it warm up for about 10 minutes. Preheat the oven to 375°. Roll the dough to a ¼-inch thickness between two pieces of wax paper or plastic wrap lightly dusted with flour. Cut the cookie dough into 3¼-inch-tall triangles. Place on cookie sheets lined with parchment paper. Insert a craft stick three quarters of the way under each cookie.

5. Bake for 10 to 12 minutes, or until the cookies start to brown lightly around the edges. Let the cookies cool for 5 minutes on the sheet before transferring them to a cooling rack. Frost and decorate the cookies after they have cooled completely.

chunky chocolate bark

TOTAL TIME: 40 MINUTES (plus chill time) | **MAKES:** 1¾ POUNDS

Once you've sampled this melt-in-your-mouth confection, you'll be tempted to fill your own candy dish with it instead of giving it away.

YOU WILL NEED

- ❑ 1 cup shelled pistachio nuts
  (about ½ pound in shell)
- ❑ 12 ounces semisweet chocolate, chopped
- ❑ 8 ounces white chocolate, chopped
- ❑ ¾ cup dried, sweetened cranberries

1. Heat the oven to 350° and lightly toast the pistachio nuts on a baking sheet, about 10 minutes, stirring occasionally. Let the nuts cool.

2. Melt the semisweet chocolate in the top of a double boiler set over simmering water, stirring until smooth. You can also microwave it in a dry, microwave-safe bowl, uncovered, on medium power for 2 to 3 minutes, stirring once. Remove the chocolate from the microwave and stir until smooth. Melt the white chocolate separately, following the same directions.

3. In a small bowl, combine the nuts and cranberries. Stir half of them into the semisweet chocolate. Using a spatula, spread the mixture to about a ½-inch thickness on a large cookie sheet. Drop tablespoons of the white chocolate over the dark chocolate. With the tip of a butter knife, swirl the chocolates together to create a marbled effect. Sprinkle on the remaining nuts and berries.

4. Refrigerate the bark for about 1 hour or until firm and then break it into pieces. Store the bark in an airtight container in the refrigerator for up to a month.

peppermint patties

TOTAL TIME: 1 HOUR (Plus cooling time) | **MAKES:** 5 DOZEN

These are the addictive classics, with a snappy minty middle and a luscious chocolate coating.

YOU WILL NEED

- ❏ 2 tablespoons plus 1 teaspoon water
- ❏ 1 tablespoon light corn syrup
- ❏ 1 teaspoon fresh lemon juice
- ❏ 1 teaspoon peppermint extract
- ❏ 1 (1-pound) box confectioners' sugar

- ❏ 1 tablespoon shortening
- ❏ 10 to 12 ounces semisweet or bittersweet chocolate chips
- ❏ 6 hard mint candies (we used Starlight), crushed in a Ziploc bag with a rolling pin

1. In a bowl, stir together the water, corn syrup, lemon juice, and peppermint extract, then sift in half the confectioners' sugar. Add the shortening. With an electric mixer, beat on medium, then slowly sift in the remaining confectioners' sugar until the mixture is well combined.

2. Knead the mixture into a ball (it will be very stiff; if necessary, add ½ teaspoon water to make it workable). Use the bottom of a glass pie plate to apply firm, even pressure to flatten the ball between sheets of wax paper into a circle about 9 inches in diameter and ¼ inch thick. Lay the wax-paper-covered disk on a cookie sheet and freeze it until it's firm, about 15 minutes.

3. Place the frozen disk on a cutting surface and remove and reserve the waxed paper. Cover a cookie sheet with parchment paper. With a small round cutter (ours was 1¼ inches), cut out circles from the disk, then place them on the cookie sheet. Gather the scraps into a ball, use the pie plate and wax paper to flatten it again, and cut more circles until the entire disk is used up. Freeze the circles for 10 minutes.

4. Meanwhile, melt the chocolate in the top of a double boiler over barely simmering water. Coat the patties one at a time: balance each on a fork and dip it (use another fork as needed to flip the patty in the chocolate), then shake off any excess chocolate before returning the coated patty to the parchment paper. Sprinkle each patty with a bit of crushed mint candy. Add more chocolate to the double boiler as necessary until all the patties are coated.

5. Harden the finished patties in the refrigerator for at least an hour, preferably overnight.

pretty peppermint sticks

TOTAL TIME: 20 MINUTES (plus cooling time)

In a small bowl, microwave 1 cup chocolate chips and 1 teaspoon vegetable oil for 1 minute. Continue heating in 10-second bursts, stirring between heatings. When most, but not all, of the chips have melted, stir the chocolate until it is smooth. Spread white nonpareils on a sheet of wax paper. Dip one end of a peppermint stick into the chocolate, then roll it in the nonpareils. Set each stick on another sheet of wax paper until the chocolate has set, about 1 hour. Place sets of five candies in clear cellophane bags, staple them closed and affix decorative labels.

white chocolate snowballs

TOTAL TIME: 30 MINUTES (plus cooling times) | **MAKES:** 48 SNOWBALLS

A delicious blend of salty and sweet makes these white chocolate peanut butter balls taste as good as they look.

YOU WILL NEED

❏ 1½ cups peanut butter
❏ ½ cup (1 stick) butter, softened
❏ 1 (16-ounce) package confectioners' sugar
❏ 2 cups white chocolate chips
❏ 1 tablespoon vegetable shortening
❏ ½ cup shelled, unsalted peanuts

1. Line a large baking sheet with aluminum foil and another with wax paper. Set both aside. Using an electric mixer (or a wooden spoon), beat together the peanut butter and butter in a large bowl until blended and smooth. Add the sugar, ½ cup at a time and blend until smooth.

2. Press the mixture into 1-inch balls. The dough will be dry, so it may be easier to form with damp hands. Place the balls on the foil-lined sheet. Let stand until firm, about 30 minutes.

3. Melt the white chocolate chips and shortening in a double boiler or heatproof bowl set atop a pot of simmering water over medium-high heat. Stir continuously until smooth. Remove the pan from the heat. Using a toothpick for a handle, pierce each ball, then dip it into the melted chocolate. Spoon chocolate over the balls to coat them, if needed. Set them on the wax-paper-lined sheet and top each with a peanut half. Refrigerate until set, about 30 minutes. Store in an airtight container in the refrigerator.

peanut butter toffee bars

TOTAL TIME: 45 MINUTES (plus cooling time) | **MAKES:** 39 1" x 3" bars

This tempting gift deliciously combines three classic candy bar flavors.

YOU WILL NEED

- ½ cup butter, at room temperature
- ½ cup creamy peanut butter
- ¾ cup packed brown sugar
- 1 large egg yolk
- 1½ cups flour
- ½ cup quick oats
- ¼ teaspoon salt
- 3 cups dark or semisweet chocolate chips
- 1 cup toffee baking pieces

1. Heat the oven to 350°. Line a 9- by 13-inch baking pan with foil so that the ends extend over the edges of the pan by at least 2 inches.

2. In the large bowl of an electric mixer, beat the butter, peanut butter, sugar, and egg yolk on medium-high speed until the mixture is smooth and creamy, about 2 minutes, scraping down the sides of the bowl if necessary. Add the flour, oats, and salt and beat the mixture on low until the ingredients are just blended, about 30 seconds.

3. Press the mixture evenly into the bottom of the prepared pan. Bake the crust until it is golden brown, 15 to 20 minutes (be careful not to overbake).

4. Remove the pan from the oven and scatter the chocolate chips evenly over the crust. Return the pan to the oven for 1 minute. Remove the pan again and, using a small offset spatula, spread the chocolate evenly over the crust.

5. Sprinkle the toffee pieces over the chocolate, gently pressing them into place.

6. Set the pan on a wire rack to cool until the chocolate has set, about 2 hours. Using the edges of the foil, lift the dessert from the pan, then cut it into rectangles.

peppermint tree

TOTAL TIME: 1 HOUR | **MAKES:** 1 TREE

With green mint boughs and sour ball lights, this tabletop tree is a treat for kids to decorate.

YOU WILL NEED

- ❑ Double-sided foam tape
- ❑ 9- by 4-inch Styrofoam cones (sold in most craft stores)
- ❑ 3 10-ounce bags of individually wrapped green striped mints
- ❑ Small bag of individually wrapped multicolored sour balls or jawbreakers
- ❑ Yellow paper
- ❑ Yellow lollipop
- ❑ Decorative candle stand

1. Apply strips of double-sided foam tape to the Styrofoam cone, as shown below, until virtually the entire surface is covered.

2. Now your child can attach the wrapped mints to the exposed tape, starting with one row around the bottom and working his way up. For the best coverage and color, he should stick each mint to the tree by the rounded edge rather than with the flat surface facing out. Encourage him to mix in a few multicolored sour ball or jawbreaker lights as he goes.

3. For a tree topper, cut a star out of the yellow paper, tape the lollipop to it, and then push the lollipop stick straight down into the cone. Set the tree on the decorative candle stand.

chocolate fondue

TOTAL TIME: 15 MINUTES | **SERVES:** 6-8

This sweet dessert is quick and easy to assemble, and everyone will enjoy skewering their own selection of fruits and dipping them into the melted chocolate.

YOU WILL NEED

FOR THE FRUIT DIPPERS

❑ 1 pint fresh strawberries
❑ 1 cup fresh pineapple
❑ 2 bananas
❑ 2 cups store-bought angel food cake
❑ Wooden skewers

FOR THE CHOCOLATE SAUCE

❑ 12 ounces semisweet chocolate chips
❑ ⅔ cup heavy cream

1. Wash the strawberries and cut off the tops.

2. Cut the pineapple, bananas, and angel food cake into chunks.

3. Pat the strawberries and pineapple chunks dry with a paper towel.

4. Warm the chocolate chips and heavy cream in a fondue pot (or in the microwave).

5. Arrange all of your goodies in separate bowls along with wooden skewers for dipping.

hot chocolate bar

Prepare plenty of **hot cocoa** from your favorite recipe or mix and keep it toasty in a thermos jug. Set out dishes of **mini marshmallows, white chocolate chips,** and **crushed peppermints** so your guests can customize their drinks to their own sweet specifications.

chocolate mug cakes

TOTAL TIME: 45 MINUTES | SERVES: 12

Bake your favorite chocolate cake batter in individual mugs for a warming winter dessert.

YOU WILL NEED
❑ Cooking spray
❑ Chocolate cake batter
❑ Marshmallow creme
❑ Oven-safe mugs

1. Coat the insides of oven safe mugs with cooking spray, then fill the mugs halfway with chocolate cake batter. We used a mix for German chocolate cake, which is a lighter color than regular chocolate cake and looks more like hot cocoa.

2. Follow the cupcake baking instructions on the cake mix package. The cakes are done when a toothpick inserted into the center of one comes out clean or with just a few crumbs. Allow the cakes to cool for about 15 minutes.

3. Top each mug with a generous dollop of marshmallow creme and serve with a spoon. One cake mix makes enough batter for 12 of our mugs; if you want fewer than a dozen, bake the remaining batter in a small pan.